Space
Word Problems Starring
Ratios
and
Proportions

Rebecca

Wingard-Nelson

Enslow Elementary, an imprint of Enslow Publishers, Inc.

Enslow Elementary® is a registered trademark of Enslow Publishers, Inc.

Library of Congress Cataloging-in-Publication Data

Wingard-Nelson, Rebecca.
  Space word problems starring ratios and proportions : math word problems solved / Rebecca Wingard-Nelson.
     p. cm. — (Math word problems solved)
  Includes bibliographical references and index.
  Summary: "Explores methods of solving ratios and proportions word problems using space examples"—Provided by publisher.
  ISBN-13: 978-0-7660-2921-7
  ISBN-10: 0-7660-2921-2
  1. Ratio and proportion—Juvenile literature. 2. Word problems (Mathematics)—Juvenile literature. 3. Astronomy—Juvenile literature. I. Title.
  QA117.W5674 2009
  513.2'4—dc22
                2008030785

Printed in the United States of America

10 9 8 7 6 5 4 3 2 1

To Our Readers: We have done our best to make sure all Internet Addresses in this book were active and appropriate when we went to press. However, the author and the publisher have no control over and assume no liability for the material available on those Internet sites or on other Web sites they may link to. Any comments or suggestions can be sent by e-mail to comments@enslow.com or to the address on the back cover.

♻ Enslow Publishers, Inc., is committed to printing our books on recycled paper. The paper in every book contains 10% to 30% post-consumer waste (PCW). The cover board on the outside of each book contains 100% PCW. Our goal is to do our part to help young people and the environment too!

Illustrations: Tom LaBaff

Cover illustration: Tom LaBaff

Free Worksheets are available for this book at http://www.enslow.com. Search for the **Math Word Problems Solved** series name. The publisher will provide access to the worksheets for five years from the book's first publication date.

Contents

Introduction

"Why do I have to do math?"

    Math is used in your life every day.

    Word problems show you some of the ways.

"But I hate word problems."

    You use word problems all the time, and you

    probably don't even realize it.

"The stories in word problems would never happen!"

    Sometimes math word problems don't look very real.

    A lot of real-life word problems are very hard to solve.

    For now, have fun getting started on word problems

    about space.

"How can this book help me?"

    This book will give you helpful tips for solving

    word problems. Learn how to understand the

    question, how to plan a way to solve it, and how to

    check your answer. You'll see that word problems

    really are "no problem" after all!

Problem-Solving Tips

Word problems might be part of your homework, on a test, or in your life. These tips can help you solve them, no matter where they show up.

Be positive!

When you get a problem right the first time, good for you! When you don't get a problem right the first time, but you learn from your mistakes, AWESOME for you! You learned something new!

Get help early!

New problems build on old ones. If you don't understand today's problem, tomorrow's problem will be even harder to understand.

Do your homework!

The more you practice anything, the better you become at it. You can't play an instrument or play a sport well without practice. Homework problems are your practice.

Move on!

If you get stuck, move on to the next problem. Do the problems you know how to solve first. You'll feel more confident. And you won't miss the ones you know because you ran out of time. Go back later and try the problems you skipped.

Ask questions!
When someone is helping you, asking good questions tells the person what you don't understand. If you don't ask questions, you will never get answers!

 ### Take a break!
If you have tried everything you can think of but are only getting frustrated, take a break. Close your eyes and take a deep breath. Stretch your arms and legs. Get a drink of water or a snack. Then come back and try again.

 ### Don't give up!
The first time you try to solve a word problem, you might come up with an answer that does not make sense. Don't give up! Check your math. Try solving the problem a different way. If you quit, you won't learn.

All About Ratios

Ratios compare numbers.

There were 35 astronauts selected to enter NASA's space program in 1978. Of these, 6 were female and 29 were male.

Ratios can compare two parts of something, such as female to male astronauts (6 to 29), or a part and a whole, such as female astronauts to all astronauts (6 to 35). Ratios can even compare related, but different, things—like a number of astronauts and how much food they eat each day.

Ratios can be written in three ways.

Using the word "to"	Using a colon	Using a fraction bar
6 to 29	6 : 29	$\dfrac{6}{29}$

The numbers in a ratio are called terms. In the ratio 6 : 29, the first term is 6, and the second term is 29.

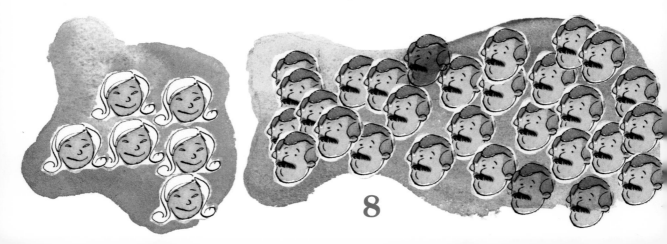

8

Proportions compare two ratios.

On Mars you weigh only 1 pound for every 3 pounds you weigh on Earth. That means if you weigh 50 pounds on Mars, you weigh 150 pounds on Earth.

A proportion uses the equal sign to show that two ratios have the same value.

$$\frac{3 \text{ pounds}}{1 \text{ pound}} = \frac{150 \text{ pounds}}{50 \text{ pounds}}$$

Rates are special ratios.

The average cost of a space shuttle mission is $450 million.

Rates use the word "per" or a fraction bar to compare numbers with different units, like dollars and missions. Some other examples of rates are "dollars per pound" and "miles per hour."

The cost of a space shuttle mission is

$450 million per mission, or
$450 million/mission.

Problem-Solving Steps

Word problems can be solved by following four easy steps.

Here's the problem.

A five-day spaceflight is being planned. Each astronaut can pick 2 snacks per day. At this rate, how many snacks can each astronaut choose for the entire flight?

(1) **Read and understand the problem.**
Read the problem carefully.
Ask yourself questions, like:

What do you know?
The spaceflight is 5 days long.
Each astronaut can choose 2 snacks per day.

What are you trying to find?
How many snacks each astronaut can choose.

What kind of problem is this?
This is a rate problem *(see pp. 28–29)*. The rate is 2 snacks per day. This rate problem gives you the rate of snacks for one day, and wants you to find the number of snacks for 5 days. It is a multiplication problem.

② Make a plan.

Some problems tell you how they should be solved. They may say "draw a picture" or "make a table." For other problems, you need to make your own plan. Use whatever plan makes the most sense and is easiest for you. Some plans you might try are:

Look for a pattern
Estimate
Guess and check
Make a list
Make a drawing

Write an equation
Use a model
Break it apart
Use a table
Use logical reasoning

How can you solve this problem?
You can write a multiplication equation.

③ Solve the problem.

It is time to do the math! If you find that your plan is not working, make a new plan. Don't give up the first time. Write your answer. Make sure you include the units.

Let's write the equation.
Multiply the number of days by the number of snacks per day.

$$\begin{array}{r} 5 \text{ days} \\ \times\ 2 \text{ snacks per day} \\ \hline 10 \text{ snacks} \end{array}$$

Each astronaut can choose 10 snacks.

④ Look back.

The problem is solved!
But you aren't finished yet.
Take a good look at your answer.
Does it make sense? Did you include the units?
Did you use the right numbers to begin?
Estimate or use the inverse operation to check
your math. Is there another plan you could have
used to solve the problem?

Did you include the units in your answer? Yes.

Could you have solved the problem another way?
Yes. You could draw a picture to show 2 snacks
each day for 5 days. Then count the total number
of snacks.

Day 1	Day 2	Day 3	Day 4	Day 5

There are 10 snacks in all.

Astronauts eat
tortillas instead of
bread in space.
Bread crumbs can
float around and
end up in equipment,
or in the eyes, ears, and
noses of astronauts.

13

Read a Table

Sometimes you need to use information from a table to solve a problem.

Here's the problem.

There are 8 planets in our solar system. Some of the planets are made of rock. Others are made of gas. Use the table to find the ratio of the planets made of rock to the total planets in our solar system.

Planet	Material
Earth	rock
Jupiter	gas
Mars	rock
Mercury	rock
Neptune	gas
Saturn	gas
Uranus	gas
Venus	rock

Read and understand.

What do you know?
The planets in our solar system are made of rock or gas.

What are you trying to find?
The ratio of planets made of rock to total planets in our solar system.

Plan.

Use the table to find the number of planets that are made of rock. Then write a ratio.

14

Solve.

This ratio compares the number of planets made of rock to the total number of planets in our solar system. Use the table to count the number of planets that are made of rock.

4 planets—Earth, Mars, Mercury, and Venus—are made of rock.

The problem tells you there are 8 planets in our solar system.

For our solar system, the ratio of planets made of rock to total planets is 4 to 8.

Look back.

Did you answer the right question? Yes.

Could you have answered in a different way? Yes. Ratios can be written using a colon, 4:8, or using a fraction bar, $\frac{4}{8}$.

Comparison Sentences

A ratio in fraction form can be used in a comparison sentence.

Here's the problem.

The distance from Earth to the Sun is called an astronomical unit (AU). Neptune is 30 AUs from the Sun. Write a sentence using the words "as far as" to compare the distances from Neptune and Earth to the Sun.

Read and understand.
What do you know?
Earth is one AU from the Sun.
Neptune is 30 AUs from the Sun.

What are you trying to find?
A sentence that uses "as far as" to compare the distances from Earth and Neptune to the Sun.

Plan.
A ratio can be written as a fraction. The fraction can be used in a sentence to compare the two distances. Let's write a ratio as a fraction, then write a sentence.

Solve.

Write the ratio.

$$\frac{\text{distance in AUs from Earth to the Sun}}{\text{distance in AUs from Neptune to the Sun}} \qquad \frac{1}{30}$$

Now write a sentence.

Earth is $\frac{1}{30}$ as far as Neptune from the Sun.

Look back.

What happens if you put the terms in a different order (Neptune first)?

The ratio becomes $\frac{30}{1}$, so the sentence is:

Neptune is 30 times as far as Earth from the Sun.

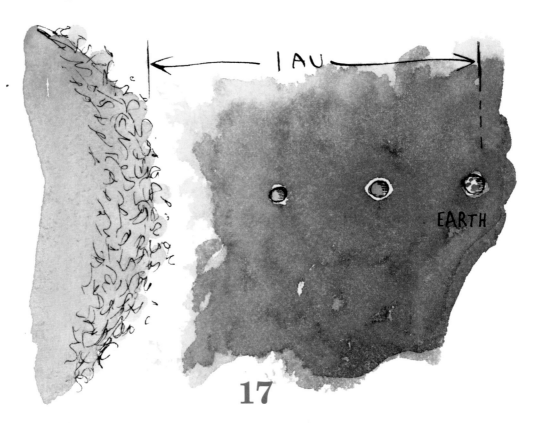

I AU

EARTH

Logical Reasoning

Although ratios can be written in fraction form, they are not fractions.

Here's the problem.

On Monday night, Kory saw 2 B stars and 28 M stars. On Tuesday night, he saw one B star and 30 M stars. Give the ratio of B stars to M stars for Monday night, Tuesday night, and the two nights combined.

Read and understand.

What do you know?
Monday night Kory saw 2 B stars and 28 M stars.
Tuesday night Kory saw 1 B star and 30 M stars.

What are you trying to find?
Three ratios:
> B to M stars on Monday night,
> B to M stars on Tuesday night, and
> B to M stars on the two nights together.

Plan.

Let's write the ratios for Monday and Tuesday night, then add to find the ratio for the two nights together.

Solve.

	Monday night:	Tuesday night:
$\dfrac{\text{B stars}}{\text{M stars}}$	$\dfrac{2}{28}$	$\dfrac{1}{30}$

Ratios are NOT added or subtracted in the same way as fractions. To find the third ratio, decide how you can find the ratio for the two nights combined. You must find the total number of B stars for both nights, and the total number of M stars for both nights.

$$\frac{\text{Monday B stars} + \text{Tuesday B stars}}{\text{Monday M stars} + \text{Tuesday M stars}} = \frac{2 + 1}{28 + 30} = \frac{3}{58}$$

The ratio of B stars to M stars for Monday night is 2 to 28. For Tuesday night it is 1 to 30. For the two nights combined it is 3 to 58.

Look back.

Did you answer all three questions? Yes.
Did you start with the right numbers? Yes.

19

Equivalent Ratios

Ratios that have the same value, such as 1 to 3 and 2 to 6, are called equivalent.

? Here's the problem.

A dog that weighs 12 pounds on Earth would weigh only 2 pounds on the Moon. Using the same ratio, how much would a person who weighs 120 pounds on Earth weigh on the Moon?

Read and understand.

What do you know?
A dog that weighs 12 pounds on Earth would weigh 2 pounds on the Moon.

What are you trying to find?
How much a person who weighs 120 pounds on Earth would weigh on the Moon.

Plan.

The problem says "using the same ratio." Let's find the ratio of the dog's weight on Earth and weight on the Moon first, then change it to match the person's weight on Earth.

Solve.

Find the ratio.

DOG: $\dfrac{\text{Earth weight}}{\text{Moon weight}}$ $\dfrac{12 \text{ pounds}}{2 \text{ pounds}}$

Change the ratio to higher terms by multiplying each term by the same number. The person weighs 120 pounds on Earth. To change Earth weight (12) to 120, you multiply by 10. Multiply each term by 10.

PERSON:

$$\frac{\text{Earth weight}}{\text{Moon weight}} \quad \frac{12 \text{ pounds} \times 10 = 120 \text{ pounds}}{2 \text{ pounds} \times 10 \ = \ 20 \text{ pounds}}$$

The person who weighs 120 pounds on Earth would weigh 20 pounds on the Moon.

Look back.

Does your answer make sense? Yes.
Why? Because the person weighs 10 times as much as the dog on Earth, and 10 times as much as the dog on the Moon.

21

Use Mental Math

When the numbers in a problem are easy to work with, you can use mental math.

Here's the problem.

One night Charla saw 40 flying objects, but could not identify 2. Write the ratio of the unidentified flying objects to the total number of flying objects she saw. Write the ratio in lowest terms.

> When Venus is bright, hundreds of people report that they see a UFO.

Read and understand.

What do you know?
Charla saw 40 flying objects.
She could not identify 2 of the flying objects.

What are you trying to find?
The ratio in lowest terms of flying objects she could not identify to flying objects she saw.

What is lowest terms?
When the ratio cannot be reduced any lower.

Plan.
Let's write the ratio, then reduce it to lowest terms.

 Solve.

Write the ratio.

flying objects not identified : flying objects in all

$$2 : 40$$

Remember, you can multiply or divide each term of a ratio by the same number without changing the value of the ratio.

Both 2 and 40 can be divided by 2 in your head.

$$2 \div 2 : 40 \div 2$$
$$1 : 20$$

The ratio of flying objects Charla could not identify to flying objects she saw is 1 : 20.

Look back.

Check the math. Use multiplication to check division. Multiply each term (1 and $1 \times 2 = 2$
20) by the number you divided by (2). $20 \times 2 = 40$
If the products are the numbers you
started with, then your math is correct.
Did you start with 2 and 40? Yes.   ✓

Use Paper and Pencil

When numbers are too hard to use in your head, you can use a paper and pencil to do the math.

Here's the problem.

A rocket uses 105 kilograms of fuel in 30 seconds. Write a rate to show how fast the fuel is used by the rocket. Make sure the rate is in lowest terms.

Read and understand.

What do you know?
The rocket uses 105 kilograms of fuel in 30 seconds.

What are you trying to find?
The rate at which the rocket uses fuel.

What is a rate?
A rate is a ratio that uses the word "per" or a fraction bar to compare numbers with different units. Some examples of rates are "dollars per pound" and "miles per hour."

Plan.

Let's write a ratio that is a rate, then reduce it to lowest terms.

Solve.

Write the rate.

$$\frac{\text{amount of fuel used}}{\text{time}} = \frac{105 \text{ kilograms}}{30 \text{ seconds}}$$

Reduce the rate to lowest terms. You can divide more than one time to get to lowest terms. If you cannot divide the numbers in your head, use a paper and pencil.

$$\frac{105 \text{ kg} \div 5}{30 \text{ s} \div 5} = \frac{21 \text{ kg} \div 3}{6 \text{ s} \div 3} = \frac{7 \text{ kg}}{2 \text{ s}}$$

$$\begin{array}{r} 21 \\ 5\overline{)105} \\ -10 \\ \hline 05 \\ -5 \\ \hline 0 \end{array}$$

The rocket uses fuel at a rate of 7 kilograms per 2 seconds.

Look back.

Is there something you could have done differently?
Yes. To reduce the rate to lowest terms, divide 105 and 30 by their greatest common factor, 15.

$$\frac{105 \text{ kg} \div 15}{30 \text{ s} \div 15} = \frac{7 \text{ kg}}{2 \text{ s}}$$

This way you only need to divide once!

Use a Calculator

When you need an accurate answer fast, or the numbers are too hard to calculate by hand, you can use a calculator.

Here's the problem.

It took a flash of light on the Moon 1.34 seconds to be seen on Earth. The Moon was 401,721 kilometers from Earth. Write a unit rate to the nearest kilometer for the speed of the light.

Read and understand.

What do you know?
From Earth, it took 1.34 seconds to see a light from the Moon.
The Moon was 401,721 kilometers from Earth.

What are you trying to find?
A unit rate for the speed of the light.

What is a unit rate?
A unit rate is a rate with one unit as the second term. Unit rates are usually written without the 1, such as 5 miles per hour instead of 5 miles per 1 hour.

What is speed?
Speed is a rate that compares distance to time.

Plan.

Write the rate for the speed.
Reduce the rate so that
1 is the second term.

Solve.

Write the rate for speed.

$$\frac{\text{distance}}{\text{time}} = \frac{401{,}721 \text{ km}}{1.34 \text{ s}}$$

To find any unit rate, you can divide each term by the second term. $401{,}721 \div 1.34$ is a hard problem, so use a calculator. Round the answer to the nearest whole number.

$$\frac{401{,}721 \text{ km} \div 1.34}{1.34 \text{ s} \div 1.34} = \frac{299{,}792 \text{ km}}{1 \text{ s}}$$

**The speed of the light is
299,792 km per second.**

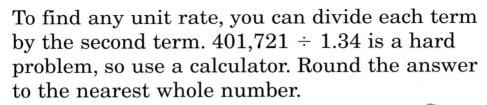

Look Back.

When is a good time to use a calculator?

1. When the problem is hard and your teacher says that you can.
2. To check your answers.
3. When you need a fast accurate answer.

Multiplying Rates

Problems that give you a rate are often multiplication or division problems.

Here's the problem.

Neptune spins at a rate of 16 hours per rotation. How many hours does Neptune take to rotate 5 times?

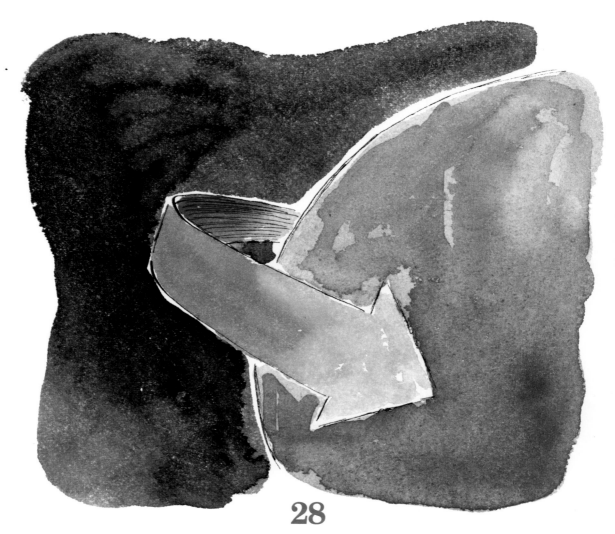

Read and understand.

What do you know?
Neptune spins at 16 hours per rotation.

What are you trying to find?
How many hours Neptune takes to rotate 5 times.

Plan.

Sixteen hours per rotation is a unit rate.
It means one rotation takes 16 hours.
To find how many hours 5 rotations take,
you can multiply. Let's write an equation.

Solve.

Multiply the number of hours one rotation takes
(16) by the number of rotations (5).

$$
\begin{array}{cc}
\overset{3}{16} & \overset{3}{16} \\
\underline{\times\ 5} & \underline{\times\ 5} \\
0 & 80
\end{array}
$$

Neptune takes 80 hours to rotate 5 times.

Look back.

Does the answer make sense? Yes.

Is there another way you can solve this problem?
Yes. You could add the time it takes for one
rotation (16 hours) five times.

$16 + 16 + 16 + 16 + 16 = 80$

Use a Formula

A formula is an equation that shows how quantities and rates are related.

? Here's the problem.

A rocket traveled at a rate of 25,000 miles per hour for 3 hours. How many miles did it travel? Use the formula *distance = speed × time*, or *d = st*.

> To orbit Earth, a space shuttle travels at about 17,500 miles per hour. To escape Earth's gravity, a rocket must travel at least 25,000 miles per hour.

Read and understand.

What do you know?
The rocket speed was 25,000 miles per hour.
The rocket traveled for 3 hours.

What are you trying to find?
The number of miles the rocket traveled.

Plan.
The problem gives you a formula to find distance.
Let's use the formula.

Solve.
Write the formula.

distance = speed × time

Put the numbers you know in the formula.

distance = 25,000 mph × 3 h

25,000 × 3 = 75,000

The rocket traveled 75,000 miles.

Look back.
Why is the answer in miles? Because the speed
was given in miles per hour, and the problem
asked for a number of miles.

Change Units

Units in a rate can be changed in the same way you convert units that are not in a rate.

 Here's the problem.

The speed of light is about 300,000 kilometers per second. What is the speed of light in kilometers per hour?

One light-year is the distance light can travel in one Earth year.

Read and understand.

What do you know?
The speed of light is 300,000 kilometers per second.

What are you trying to find?
A rate in kilometers per hour that is the same as 300,000 kilometers per second.

Plan.

Let's convert seconds to minutes, then minutes to hours.

Solve.

The original rate is 300,000 kilometers per second, or per 1 second.

There are 60 seconds in one minute. Multiply BOTH the distance (300,000 kilometers) AND the number of seconds (1) by 60.

$$\frac{300{,}000 \text{ kilometers} \times 60}{1 \text{ second} \times 60} = \frac{18{,}000{,}000 \text{ kilometers}}{60 \text{ seconds (1 minute)}}$$

Now do the same thing again. There are 60 minutes in one hour. Multiply BOTH the distance AND the number of minutes (1) by 60.

$$\frac{18{,}000{,}000 \text{ km} \times 60}{1 \text{ minute} \times 60} = \frac{1{,}080{,}000{,}000 \text{ km}}{60 \text{ minutes (1 hour)}}$$

300,000 kilometers per second is the same speed as 1,080,000,000 kilometers per hour.

Look back.

Is there another way you can solve this problem? Yes. If you know there are 3,600 seconds in one hour, you can multiply in one step instead of two.

Use a Model

Models can help you understand and solve some problems.

Here's the problem.

A teacher splits her class into groups to study Saturn and its rings. They have models in a ratio of 4 cardboard rings for every one cardboard Saturn. If they use 25 cardboard pieces in all, how many groups are there if each group gets one Saturn?

Read and understand.

What do you know?
The ratio of cardboard rings to Saturns is 4 to 1. The class is split into groups with one Saturn each. The class uses 25 cardboard pieces in all.

What are you trying to find?
The number of groups in the class.

Plan.
Let's use a model. You can use anything as a model. Beans, counters, chips, pennies, or cereal will work for this problem. Let's use beans.

Solve.

You know that 25 pieces are used in all, so start with 25 beans.

Make a group with one bean for the Saturn piece, and four beans for the ring pieces.

Keep making groups until you run out of beans.

Count the groups. There are 5.

The class is split into 5 groups.

Look back.

Check your answer.

You know each group gets one Saturn piece and 4 ring pieces, or 5 total pieces.

5 pieces for each group × 5 groups = 25 pieces

Write a Proportion

A proportion uses an equal sign to show that ratios are equal.

Here's the problem.

Mercury takes about 90 days to orbit the Sun. Venus takes about 225 days. Is 2 to 3 the correct ratio for the time it takes Mercury to orbit the Sun to the time it takes Venus to orbit the Sun?

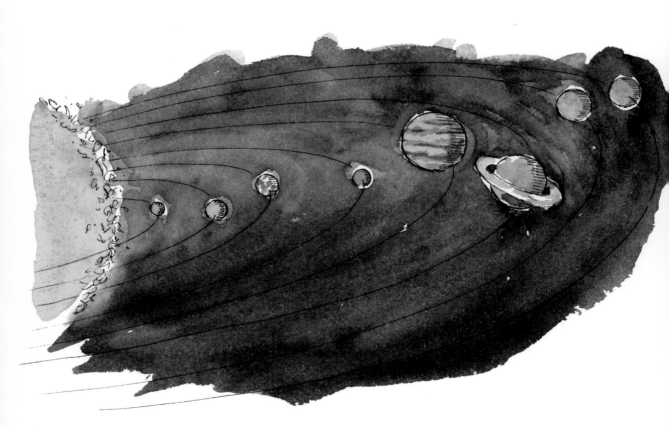

Read and understand.

What do you know?
Mercury takes 90 days to orbit the Sun.
Venus takes 225 days to orbit the Sun.

What are you trying to find?
If the ratio of orbit times for Mercury and
Venus is 2 to 3.

Plan.

A proportion is an equation with a ratio on each
side. Let's write a proportion, and see if it is true.

Solve.

Write the proportion by putting an equal sign
between what you know and what you read.

What you know:		What you read:
Mercury orbit time	$\dfrac{90 \text{ days}}{225 \text{ days}}$ $=$	$\dfrac{2}{3}$
Venus orbit time		

Are the ratios equivalent? Reduce each ratio to
lowest terms to check. You may need to reduce
more than one time to get to lowest terms.

$$\frac{90 \div 5}{225 \div 5} = \frac{18 \div 9}{45 \div 9} = \frac{2}{5} \overset{?}{\underset{\text{NO!}}{=}} \frac{2}{3}$$

**No, the ratio of times for Mercury and Venus
to orbit the Sun is not 2 to 3.**

Look back.

Did you start with the right numbers? Yes.

Scale Drawings

A scale drawing is a picture that shows objects reduced or enlarged according to a proportion.

Here's the problem.

The diameter of Mars is about 7,000 kilometers. Saturn's diameter is about 120,000 kilometers. Kyle made a scale drawing of the solar system. His drawing of Mars has a diameter of 7 millimeters. What should the diameter of his drawing of Saturn be?

Read and understand.

What do you know?
The diameter of Mars is about 7,000 km.
The diameter of Saturn is about 120,000 km.
The drawing of Mars has a diameter of 7 mm.

What are you trying to find?
What the diameter of Kyle's drawing of Saturn should be.

Plan.
Let's set up a proportion to find the missing diameter.

 Solve.

	planet diameter	model diameter
Mars	7,000 km	7 mm
Saturn	120,000 km	?

$$\frac{7{,}000 \text{ km}}{120{,}000 \text{ km}} = \frac{7 \text{ mm}}{?}$$

You can divide 7,000 by 1,000 to get 7.
Divide 120,000 by 1,000 to find the missing term.
120,000 ÷ 1,000 = 120

	planet diameter	model diameter
Mars	7,000 km	7 mm
Saturn	120,000 km	120 mm

$$\frac{7{,}000 \text{ km}}{120{,}000 \text{ km}} = \frac{7 \text{ mm}}{120 \text{ mm}}$$

Kyle's drawing of Saturn should have a diameter of 120 millimeters.

 Look back.

The units of the real planets are in kilometers, but the units in the model are in millimeters. Does that make a difference? No. The ratios are still the same.

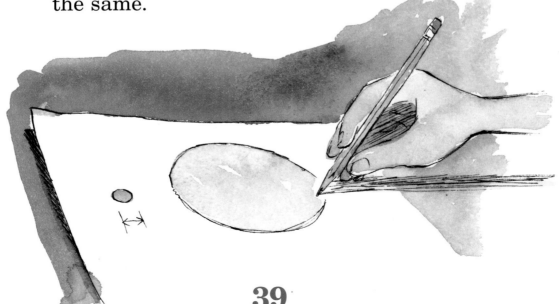

Cross Multiply

You can multiply the diagonal numbers in a proportion to see if the ratios have the same value.

Here's the problem.

For every 7 parts of Earth's surface that are covered by water, there are 3 parts covered by land. Haven is making a globe using paper squares. She has 21 blue squares for the water, and 9 green squares for the land. Are the squares in the correct ratio?

 Read and understand.
What do you know?
The ratio of water to land on Earth's surface is 7 to 3.

What are you trying to find?
If the number of blue squares (21) to green squares (9) is in the same ratio as the water to land.

 Plan.
Let's set up a proportion and check it.

Solve.

	Earth's surface		paper squares
water	$\dfrac{7}{3}$	$=$	$\dfrac{21}{9}$ (blue)
land			(green)

To check if the ratios are the same, you can cross multiply. Multiply the numbers that are diagonal to each other in the proportion.

$$\frac{7}{3} \diagdown\!\!\!\diagup \frac{21}{9} \qquad 3 \times 21 = 63$$
$$7 \times 9 = 63$$

The products are the same, so the ratios are equal.

Haven has the correct ratio of blue to green paper squares.

 Look back.

Is there another way you can check to see if the ratios are equal?

Yes. Reduce each ratio to lowest terms.

$$\frac{7}{3} \quad \text{is in lowest terms} \qquad \frac{21 \div 3}{9 \div 3} = \frac{7}{3}$$

Are the ratios equal? Yes. ✓

Scale Models

Scale models are in proportion to what they are modeling.

Here's the problem.

In a scale model of the solar system, Mercury is 2 inches from the Sun and Pluto is 204 inches from the Sun. The actual distance from Pluto to the Sun is 3,672 million miles. How many millions of miles is Mercury from the Sun?

Read and understand.

What do you know?
In the scale model, Mercury is 2 inches
and Pluto is 204 inches from the Sun.
Pluto is 3,672 million miles from the Sun.

What are you trying to find?
How far Mercury is from the Sun.

Plan.

Let's set up a proportion.

Solve.

	scale distance from Sun (inches)		actual distance from Sun (millions of miles)
Mercury	$\dfrac{2 \text{ in}}{204 \text{ in}}$	$=$	$\dfrac{?}{3{,}672}$
Pluto			

The cross products in a proportion are equal.

$$\dfrac{2}{204} \diagdown \dfrac{?}{3{,}672}$$

$204 \times ? = 7{,}344$
$2 \times 3{,}672 = 7{,}344$

Use division to find the missing number in the
multiplication problem $204 \times ? = 7{,}344$.

$7{,}344 \div 204 = 36$ $\dfrac{2}{204} = \dfrac{36}{3{,}672}$

Mercury is 36 million miles from the Sun.

Look back.

Did you start with the right numbers? Yes.
Use multiplication to check your division.
Is $204 \times 36 = 7{,}344$? Yes. ✓

43

Estimation

You can use estimation when you do not need to know the exact answer to a problem.

 Here's the problem.

Most meteorites are gray and hard. A few are black and fragile. In one area 9,146 meteorites were found. If 3 of every 1,000 meteorites found are the black fragile type, about how many of those found are the black fragile type?

 Read and understand.

What do you know?
There are 9,146 meteorites found. Three of every 1,000 meteorites found are the black fragile type.

What are you trying to find?
The number of black fragile meteorites that are found.

Is there anything special about this problem?
Yes. The problem asks "about how many."
The answer does not need to be exact.

 Plan.

Let's estimate the answer by rounding 9,146 to the greatest place value, then setting up a proportion.

44

Solve.

Round 9,146 to the thousands place.

9,146 rounds to 9,000.

Set up the proportion.

$$\frac{\text{Black, fragile}}{\text{Total}} \qquad \frac{3}{1,000} \ = \ \frac{?}{9,000}$$

1,000 multiplied by 9 is 9,000.
Multiply 3×9 to find the missing term.
$3 \times 9 = 27$

$$\frac{\text{Black, fragile}}{\text{Total}} \qquad \frac{3}{1,000} \ = \ \frac{27}{9,000}$$

About 27 of the 9,146 meteorites are the black, fragile type.

Look back.

Cross multiply to check your answer.

$$\frac{3}{1,000} \diagdown \frac{27}{9,000} \qquad \begin{array}{l} 1,000 \times 27 = 27,000 \\ 3 \times 9,000 = 27,000 \end{array} \checkmark$$

Let's Review

To solve a word problem, follow these steps:

 ## Read and understand the problem.
Know what the problem says, and what you need to find.
If you don't understand, ask questions before you start.

 ## Make a plan.
Choose the plan that makes the most sense and is easiest
for you. Remember, there is usually more than one way
to find the right answer.

 ## Solve the problem.
Use the plan. If your first plan isn't working, try a different
one. Take a break and come back with a fresh mind.

 ## Look back.
Read the problem again. Make sure your answer makes
sense. Check your math. If the answer does not look right,
don't give up now! Use what you've learned to go back and
try the problem again.

Further Reading

Clemson, David, and Wendy Clemson. *Rocket to the Moon.* Strongsville, Ohio: Gareth Stevens Publishing, 2007.

McCallum, Ann. *Rabbits Rabbits Everywhere: A Fibonacci Tale.* Watertown, Mass.: Charlesbridge Publishing, 2007.

Walsh, Kieran. *Space Math.* Vero Beach, Fla.: Rourke Publishing, 2006.

Internet Addresses

Aplusmath.
   <http://www.aplusmath.com>

Coolmath Games.
   <http://www.coolmath-games.com>

NASA.
   <http://www.nasa.gov/audience/forstudents/
      index.html>

Index